THE HISPANIC INFLUENCE IN THE UNITED STATES

LATINOS
IN AMERICAN HISTORY

JOVITA
IDAR

BY KAREN BUSH GIBSON

Mitchell Lane
PUBLISHERS

P.O. Box 619
Bear, Delaware 19701

THE HISPANIC INFLUENCE IN THE UNITED STATES

LATINOS
IN AMERICAN HISTORY

OTHER TITLES IN THE SERIES

Visit us on the web: www.mitchelllane.com
Comments? email us: mitchelllane@mitchelllane.com

THE HISPANIC INFLUENCE IN THE UNITED STATES

LATINOS

IN AMERICAN HISTORY

JOVITA
IDAR

BY KAREN BUSH GIBSON

Printing   1   2   3   4   5   6   7   8

Library of Congress Cataloging-in-Publication Data

Gibson, Karen Bush.
     Jovita Idar/Karen Bush Gibson.
       p. cm. — (Latinos in American history)
     Includes bibliographical references and index.
     ISBN 1-58415-151-x (lib bdg.)
     1. Idar, Jovita, 1885-1946. 2. Mexican American women—Texas—Biography 3. Women civil rights workers—Texas—Biography. 4. Mexican Americans—Texas—Biography. 5. Civil rights workers—Texas—Biography. 6. Mexican Americans—Civil rights—Texas—History—20th century. 7. Mexican Americans—Texas—Social conditions—20th century. 8. Texas—Ethnic relations. 9. Laredo (Tex.)—Biography. I. Title. II. Series.
F391.I33 G53 2002
323'.092—dc21
    [B]   2002022143

ABOUT THE AUTHOR: Karen Bush Gibson is a freelance writer who has written for such publications as *Boys' Life* and *Cobblestone*. She is also the author of 15 books for children and this is her first book for Mitchell Lane Publishers, Inc. Karen lives in Oklahoma with her husband and their three children.

PHOTO CREDITS: NOTE: Many of the photographs in this book were taken in black and white. Some have been hand colored for visual effect and may not accurately reflect the original colors. Cover: The Woman's Collection/Texas Woman's University; p. 6 Corbis; p. 10 The Woman's Collection/Texas Woman's University; p. 15 AP Photo; pp. 16, 18, 23, 24 Institute of Texan Cultures; p. 26 Corbis; pp. 27, 29 Institute of Texan Cultures; pp. 30, 32 The Woman's Collection/Texas Woman's University; p. 36 Barbara Marvis; p. 39 Institute of Texan Cultures; p. 41 Wayne State University.

PUBLISHER'S NOTE: This story is based on the author's extensive research, which she believes to be accurate. Any websites referenced in this publication were active as of the date of publication. Because of the fleeting nature of web sites, we cannot guarantee they will all work when you are reading this book.

CONTENTS

CHAPTER 1

CHAPTER 2

CHAPTER 3

CHAPTER 4

CHAPTER 5

CHAPTER 6

Texas cavalrymen stand over the dead body of a Tejano. The Anglos on horseback pursued the man and killed him in their own brand of justice, 1912. Crimes such as this one against people of Hispanic origin living in the United States were widespread in the early part of the twentieth century. Jovita Idar wrote about many such injustices and worked tirelessly to improve the treatment and way of life for all Hispanic Americans. (This original black & white photograph has been hand colored.)

FOR THE PEOPLE

On a warm summer day in south Texas in 1911, 14-year-old Antonio Gómez walked into a store. He was immediately ordered to leave. Antonio wasn't welcome in many stores or restaurants in his hometown of Thorndale. Neither were his family or friends. Business owners posted signs in their windows about people, such as Antonio, who had dark skin and spoke Spanish. The signs read, "No Mexicans Allowed."

Antonio refused to leave on this particular June day. Perhaps he felt he had as much right to be there as any other Texan. A fight broke out between Antonio and a man. After awhile, the man lay dead from a knife wound. Law officers arrested Antonio immediately, but before they could reach the sheriff's office, a group of Anglo men forced Antonio away from the law officers. The dead man was a Texan, an Anglo of German descent.

No trial was held for Antonio. The men beat Antonio to death. Afterwards, a buggy dragged his body through town as a warning to other Texans of Mexican descent. Police never held an investigation or arrested anyone for lynching a 14-year old boy.

Lynching, or killing someone in a violent way without a legal trial, had been around since the time of the American Revolution. During the Civil War, lynching was used against white abolitionists and African-Americans. Lynching of Mexican Americans in Texas increased after the Civil War when more Anglos from southern states settled in Texas. Police rarely arrested people who committed lynching.

Being victims of violence angered many people in south Texas; people whose families had lived on the same land long before the Anglo settlers moved to the Rio Grande Valley. These U.S. citizens were Texans of Mexican descent. They called themselves Tejanos, a term that began in the 1820s. And Tejanos worried that they too would be lynched if they spoke up. Tejanos had already suffered many injustices since Texas became part of the United States in 1845. Anglos stole ranches and farms Mexican families owned for more than 100 years.

This injustice bothered a young Mexican American woman, a third generation Texan, that people such as her were treated poorly because of their Hispanic heritage. This woman's name was Jovita Idar (hoe-VEE-ta EE-dahr), and she was a journalist. Seven months earlier, another young man named Antonio Rodríguez was accused of killing an Anglo woman in Rocksprings, Texas. Again, police did not investigate the death. Instead, townspeople took matters into their own hands and burned this 20-year-old ranch hand at the stake.

Jovita covered the incident in a Laredo, Texas newspaper called *La Crónica* by writing, "The crowd cheered when the flames engulfed his body. They did not even turn away at the smell of his burning flesh and I wondered if they even knew his name. There are so many dead that sometimes I can't remember all their names."

Jovita often wrote about discrimination and how attitudes needed to change toward Hispanics. More than a journalist, Jovita was a civil rights activist for Hispanic people. She took action to bring about changes. She formed organizations and made speeches calling for equal education, equal pay, and an end to the violence. An early feminist concerned with the rights of women, Jovita also supported more political power for Mexican Americans.

Jovita worked to better the lives of Mexicans and Texans of Mexican descent in any way she could. A special concern of hers was education. Tejano children weren't allowed to attend public schools that Anglos attended. They were segregated, so Jovita opened free kindergartens primarily for Hispanics in Texas, and taught in both Spanish and English.

When the Mexican Revolution began, Jovita crossed the Rio Grande River into Mexico and helped form a nursing corps. This organization, similar to the Red Cross, provided nursing care and helped the victims of war. Jovita put herself in danger time after time as a nurse and as an activist.

Journalist, teacher, political activist, nurse, Jovita was all these and more. She was a woman who helped those in need and fought against injustice. According to a Hispanic News Service, *La Voz de Aztlan* (Vol. 1, Issue 5; February 27, 2000) this amazing woman worked "por la raza y para la raza." She worked by the people and for the people.■

Jovita Idar, a third generation Texan, was bothered that people like her were treated badly because of their Hispanic heritage. She was a civil rights activist for Hispanic Americans.

LIVING IN TWO CULTURES

The border town of Laredo, Texas was a town of many contrasts in the latter part of the 19th century. It was a U.S. city with a strong Hispanic influence. Churches nearly 100 years old sat close to the newest transportation, the railroad. In 1885, Laredo was a frontier town of ranches and a modern enterprising community focused on commerce.

On the seventh day of that year, Jovita Idar became the second of eight children born to Nicasio Idar and Jovita Vivero de Idar. Jovita Vivero de Idar raised her family with faith and intelligence. Although named after her mother, the younger Jovita took after her activist father in many ways. Nicasio, born in December of 1855 in Point Isabel, Texas, was educated in the coastal town of Corpus Christi before moving in 1880 to Laredo on the U.S-Mexico border. A journalist and printer, Nicasio also served as assistant city marshal and justice of the peace in his adopted home of Laredo.

Soon after Jovita's father moved to Laredo, the railroads did also. Laredo's location became even more important as a hub where all roads in the area met. The first international bridge between the United States and Mexico was a temporary railroad structure with a more permanent bridge built when Jovita was four years old. Today, Laredo is considered a major gateway into Mexico.

The oldest independent settlement in Texas, Laredo enjoys a colorful history. Originally named San Agustin de Laredo after a town on the north coast of Spain, this city was founded on the banks of the Rio Grande River in 1755 as part of Spain's plan to colonize the New World. The first Spanish settlers operated ranches that raised cattle, oxen, horses, sheep, goats, and mules. Ranches sprouted up throughout the Rio Grande Valley as cattle drives and the cowboy became staples of Laredo during the 18th century.

After Mexico gained independence from Spain in 1821, Laredo became a city of Mexico. During this time, the growing community began successfully trading animal hides and wool with Mexico until Comanche and Apache raids became a danger for the people of Laredo. Not only were their lives at risk, but the raids deterred trading and ranching. The people appealed to the Mexican government for help, but being so far from the capitol of Mexico City, Laredo was largely ignored.

The Republic of Texas formed and became independent of Mexico in 1836, although Laredo still claimed loyalty to Mexico. When the United States annexed Texas in 1845, a war with Mexico followed. The United States' claim on land that historically belonged to Mexico angered Mexican authorities. The War with Mexico was fought throughout what is now the southwestern United States, but California, New Mexico, and Texas were affected the most.

When the war ended, a peace treaty called the Treaty of Guadalupe Hidalgo declared the Rio Grande River as the border between Texas and Mexico. The Rio Grande starts in southwestern Colorado's San Juan Mountains and runs through New Mexico until it reaches the Texas-Mexico border. The river follows the border of both countries for 1,241 miles before emptying into the Gulf of Mexico. This treaty effectively cut Laredo in half. South of the Rio Grande became known as Nuevo Laredo, Mexico while north of the river was Laredo, later named the seat of Webb County, in the new state of Texas.

The influences of Mexican and American ways of life were obvious in the language and architecture of Laredo. The most prominent people, usually old ranching families, lived around the San Agustin Plaza in the central part of town where both adobe and stone buildings stood. Neighborhoods, or barrios, where Spanish was the main language developed on the outskirts of central Laredo. For a period of time, Laredo was the largest Mexican city in the United States. And in the 19th century, Texas had the largest Mexican population plus shared the longest border with Mexico.

Laredo had been a city of Spain, Mexico, and finally United States in the span of a century. The changing governments might have confused residents, but little changed for the people of Laredo, at first. They were still in danger from Indian raids. Laredo court cases were often in Spanish in the early years of statehood. Tejanos even served on juries, which was illegal in other parts of Texas. Unfortunately, life for Hispanics changed once again as Anglos discovered opportunities for ranching and trading in border towns, such as Laredo.

The Treaty of Guadalupe Hidalgo also promised that Mexican Americans had rights including freedom of worship and property ownership. The treaty failed to address the differences, however, between Anglo and Mexican cultures. Mexicans Americans believed families who had always lived on a property owned that property. Pieces of paper called land deeds to prove ownership or land boundaries were not as meaningful as tradition. People owned land because their father owned it, and their father's father owned it, and so on. Furthermore, Mexican culture believed land should benefit the community at large. This idea clashed with the Anglo attitude of individuals owning and exploiting land for profit. Many Tejanos lost their land because they couldn't prove they owned it. Tejanos had few rights, and those they once had, they were losing.

One of Nicasio Idar's heroes was Abraham Lincoln. Not only had Lincoln opposed the Mexican War, he was a self-educated man who addressed problems. Nicasio, such as Lincoln, believed in fairness. Jovita's father felt it was his duty to report the problems Tejanos faced. As editor of a weekly Spanish language newspaper, *La Crónica,* in the 1890s, Nicasio published articles about abuse and discrimination against Hispanics. The banner of the newspaper proclaimed its dedication to the betterment of the Mexican-Texan people.

The Idar home placed great importance on education for both boys and girls. As a Mexican American, Jovita probably attended segregated schools and knew firsthand they were inferior to the Anglo schools. A lively and imaginative student, Jovita used her father's library to make up for educational deficits at school. Jovita spent many hours with poetry, literature, and history. She began to write poetry and even won prizes for it.

Another part of Jovita's education took place at the dinner table when family members engaged in debates about problems Tejanos suffered in south Texas. Jovita

One of Nicasios's heroes was Abraham Lincoln. Lincoln had opposed the Mexican War and he believed in fairness. This undated painting by Schapel (which has been hand colored) shows Abraham Lincoln with his wife, Mary Todd Lincoln, and their two sons, Robert Todd and Thomas Lincoln.

learned that Tejanos did not receive the same opportunities as Anglos in education or employment. She heard stories about violence against people who were Mexican. And Jovita learned about activism by watching her father advocate for Mexican American people. In addition to his work as a journalist, Nicasio was also active with labor organization according to the Texas State Historical Association. Activities, such as the ones in which Nicasio participated, were dangerous for Mexican American people in the early 20th century. Although Nicasio must have encountered threats for his beliefs, he held fast to his focus on fairness for all people.

As a teenager, Jovita translated legal papers for Laredo lawyers. She learned a great deal about the legal system from this experience. This knowledge served her well throughout her life. Later, Jovita attended a Methodist school in Laredo called the Holding Institute where she was

FORM B.   1350-702-4m.

TEACHER'S CERTIFICATE,

COUNTY.

OFFICE OF COUNTY SUPERINTENDENT.

Laredo P. O., _Webb_ County, Texas.

Whereas, _Miss Jovita Idar_

has furnished such evidence of good moral character and of ability to speak and use the English language as is required by law, *

_____ and

Whereas, _she_ has passed the required examination, and

Whereas, the County Board of Examiners have made me a sworn report stating that _she_

has made the required grades and average and possesses the other qualifications prescribed by law, and recommending

that _she_ should receive this certificate;

Now, Therefore, I, _B. Richardson_, County _Superintendent_

of _Webb_ County, State of Texas, being fully satisfied that the requirements of the law

have been complied with, do hereby grant and issue unto said _Jovita Idar_

this Teacher's Certificate of the§ _Second_ grade, which shall authorize the employment

of said holder hereof as a teacher in the public schools for ~~white~~ ~~colored~~ children of said _Webb_ County,

State of Texas.

This Certificate shall be valid in said County† _for four years_

after date of issue unless sooner cancelled by lawful authority.

Witness my official signature this the _20th_ day _June_ 190_3_.

B. Richardson

County _Supdt_ of _Webb_ County, Texas.

* In case of permanent certificate insert "and has furnished satisfactory evidence that he (or she) has taught successfully in the schools of Texas for a period of not less than three years."
§ Insert "Third," "Second," "First" or "Permanent."
† Insert "for one year," "for two years," "for four years" or "during the life of said holder," as the case may require.

Jovita's teaching certificate was issued by Webb County, Texas and dated June 20, 1903. She earned this certificate a few months before her eighteenth birthday.

known for her knowledge of history. Her own love of learning influenced her choice of a career, and she earned a teaching certificate in the summer of 1903 a few months before her 18th birthday.

The certificate was a major accomplishment in more ways than one. Teaching was an acceptable vocation in Texas for women by 1900. In fact, U.S. women led the movement in the 1880s to create public kindergartens for the nation's youngest students. However, most of the schools that trained teachers only admitted Anglo students. For a Mexican American woman to attend college was almost unheard of.

Jovita's first teaching job was in a small community called Ojuelos, on the road between Laredo and Corpus Christi. Poor conditions dominated her first teaching experience. She had practically no equipment or books, not even pencils or paper. Her students came to school hungry and dressed in rags. Sometimes the school lacked money to pay for heat in winter.

Taxes supported public schools, but Jovita found that most of the tax money went to Anglo schools that refused to admit Tejano children. Failing to raise enough money to pay for supplies or to change the segregated school system, Jovita quit her job. She knew she must find a better way to improve the lives of Tejano children, and all Mexican Americans. ■

This photo of Jovita was printed on a calendar for 1911 and printed on postcard stock as a New Year's card.

LA FEMINISTA

J ovita joined her father and two of her brothers, Eduardo and Clemente, at *La Crónica*. Her brothers also spent their lives working on civil rights for Mexican Americans. Clemente later became an important labor organizer. By 1910, Nicasio became publisher and owner in addition to editor of the newspaper.

The goal of *La Crónica* was to further the progress, moral and intellectual development of Mexicans living in Texas. The weekly newspaper covered local, regional, and world-wide news. Eduardo traveled throughout Texas to report on events affecting Tejanos. Jovita and Clemente wrote from Laredo. Jovita hoped writing about the obstacles Tejano children faced in getting an education would have a positive effect.

Although few women worked as journalists in Texas at the time, Jovita wasn't the first Tejana journalist. Poet Sara Estela Ramírez wrote occasionally for *La Crónica*. She also published in the early 1900s a Laredo newspaper called *The*

CHAPTER 3

Aurora, and a literary journal called *La Corregidora*, or the Corrector. The latter was named after a heroine in Mexico's quest for independence from Spain. Ramírez was also a teacher and writer who supported the causes of workers and women on both sides of the border.

During 1910 and 1911, Jovita wrote many articles about discrimination against Mexican children in Texas public schools and demanded equal educational opportunities for them. Moved by the fates of 14-year-old Gómez and 20-year-old Rodriguez, Jovita also began writing about the increase in lynching of Tejanos.

Jovita joined her father in 1911 to form the Primer Congreso Mexicanista, or the First Mexican Congress, to take action against the social injustices Mexican Americans encountered. According to the Women's Museum in Dallas, Jovita said, "There is nothing else but to organize."

The most influential Tejanos from 24 Texas communities met in Laredo from September 14 to 22 in the first civil rights convention Hispanics held in the United States. They chose the dates to highlight Mexican Independence Day on September 16. *La Crónica* publicized the event and re-printed all the speeches.

Journalists, teachers, Mexican consuls, and members of mutual aid societies participated in workshops and discussions about civil rights, unfair practices in land ownership, and segregation in education. They also talked about what they could do about the increase in police brutality, lynching, and capital punishment against Hispanics.

And for the first time in U.S. history, Mexican American women took an active role in a social and political movement. Jovita knew women were just as concerned as men about civil rights issues, so she and her family issued a special invitation for Hispanic women of Texas to attend the congress. The invitation worked. Women were well represented at the conference with speakers, such as Hortencia Mocaya, who spoke on problems of the criminal justice system and lynching.

Another conference speaker, orator Soledad de la Peña, spoke about the importance of education, saying, "It is necessary that all of us understand our duty and that we take a proper course of action. I, like you, believe the best way of compliance with our duty is to educate women, to instruct her, encourage her at the same time you respect her."

The presence of one influential woman was missed. Sara Estela Ramírez died three weeks before the conference at the young age of 29. Jovita wrote about her friend in *La Crónica*, calling her La Musa Texana, or the Texas Muse.

The needs of Hispanic women were more than could be addressed at the First Mexican Congress. La Liga Femenil Mexicanista (LFM) or the Mexican Feminist League became the first Hispanic feminist organization in the United States on October 15, 1911. Jovita, Soledad, and nine other educated and intelligent women met to discuss how they could make a difference in the lives of Tejanas. Two sisters, Andrea and Teresa Villareal, were members of the league. They later published a newspaper called *La Mujer Moderna*, or *The Modern Woman*.

Unfortunately, the work of the LFM remained separate from other feminist movements in the United States. When the women's suffrage movement officially began in the United States in 1848 at the first women's rights convention in Seneca Falls, New York, Tejanas were emerging from the middle of the War with Mexico. Mexican American feminism was different from mainstream Anglo feminism. Mainstream Anglo feminists, such as Elizabeth Cady Stanton and Susan B. Anthony, campaigned for the right to vote while Jovita and her Tejana contemporaries concentrated on the needs and rights of Mexican American families.

Tejanas, some struggling to survive, lived between two cultures and two lands. As Hispanic women, their needs were often second to those of their men. Furthermore, Hispanic women felt prejudice from leaders of the Anglo feminist movement toward non-white people, especially those who spoke a language other than English in the early 20th century.

Education and support of women and children became the league's chief goals. The league's first project provided free kindergarten and elementary education for Hispanics. Many members were teachers who taught in Spanish and included learning about Mexican culture in the curriculum. Classes were also held for Mexican American women. Jovita was quoted saying, "Educate a woman, and you educate a family."

La Crónica reported on the activities of the LFM. Jovita was the first president of the feminist league. Often meeting at the Idar home, the women focused their efforts on poor Tejanos. Fundraising became an important component of the league. By sponsoring literary readings and theatrical productions, Jovita and the other women raised money to provide school supplies plus clothing and food for needy families.

The LFM opened the door to later successful activism by women, especially in economics and labor. María Hernández , for example, of Lytle, Texas co-founded in 1929 a civil rights organization called the Orden Caballeros de América, or the Order of Knights of America. Her writings on social and political issues furthered the call for equality for Latinos throughout the United States.

Besides encouraging activism among Mexican American women, participants of the First Mexican Congress also called on newspapers to strengthen their cause. When the congress ended, Reverend Pedro Gardo made remarks *La*

Crónica later reprinted. Gardo said, "The Congreso Mexicanista can and should enhance the Mexican press of Texas. The newspaper is the scourge of the unjust and the denouncer of the abusers of office."

La Crónica took this trust from the Mexican Congress seriously. While the *Houston Post* was reporting on the Convention of Southern Planters setting a fixed price for cotton, *La Crónica* published information about the First Mexican Congress and the feminist league, a risk for the Idar family. After all, violence against Tejanos was increasing.

But the people of the First Mexican Congress had organized. And from that banding together, they found the power and courage to declare the need for change. Change came slowly, but it did come. After the conference, trade unions were organized. Jovita's father and her brother, Clemente, worked with the American Federation of Labor and the Texas Socialist Party to organize tens of thousands of Mexican Americans.

Women won the right to vote in 1920 with the passing of the 19th Amendment to the U.S. Constitution. Meanwhile, Jovita set about campaigning for the civil rights of all Hispanic people; men, women, and children.■

Jovita and her family supported union organization for Mexican Americans. This photo was taken in Laredo, Texas in 1915 with the Union of Stone Masons. Jovita is on the platform (left).

This photograph was taken in January 1914 in Nuevo Laredo, Mexico after the attack on Nuevo Laredo during the Mexican Revolution. Jovita Idar (fourth from left) was among the first medical volunteers who aided the wounded. Leonor Villegas de Magnon is standing to the left of Jovita (second from left in photo). The photo was taken outside a hospital.

REVOLUTION AT THE BORDER

In the United States, Texas shares the longest border with another country. During the 19th century, Texas also had more than its share of border conflicts and property disputes. When Mexico won its independence from Spain in 1821, border disputes increased. The Mexican War (1846-1848) was fought over one issue. Who owned land in Texas, New Mexico, Arizona, Utah, and California, plus parts of Colorado and Wyoming?

In Texas, the Mexican government believed the border should be 200 miles north at the Nueces River. The U.S. government argued the Rio Grande should be the border. After the U.S. victory, the border stood at the Rio Grande River. Perhaps, it was only natural that when the Mexican Revolution began in 1910 that conflict spilled over into border towns, such as Jovita's hometown of Laredo.

Dictator Porfirio Díaz ruled Mexico with an iron fist for more than three decades. As the election of 1910 approached, he jailed his increasingly popular opponent until after the election. After Díaz won the election, a small minority of Mexicans became powerful and rich, while most of the population found day-to-day existence more difficult. Mexican peasants and American Indians who lived in Mexico became victims of poverty. Tired of struggling for survival, they revolted against the domineering government. The peasants demanded equal rights in employment, housing, property ownership, and politics. Their struggle wasn't much different from what Jovita, and her family and friends were crusading for in Texas.

Jovita began writing articles supporting the revolution and leaders, such as General Francisco Villa. While people in Boston prepared to celebrate St. Patrick's Day in 1913, the Mexican Revolution moved into Laredo's backyard.

A woman named Leonor Villegas de Magnón, woke to the sounds of gunfire and screaming.

General Francisco "Pancho" Villa is shown here on horseback. He became a general in the Mexican Revolution of 1810 and controlled much of northern Mexico. Jovita supported General Villa.

She ran out of her home to see the chaos from a battle in Nuevo Laredo spill over the Rio Grande into Laredo. Everyone tried to flee from the fighting. It seemed anything that moved was being shot at. According to Leonor's autobiography *The Rebel*, her thoughts lay with the wounded soldiers in the streets. As bad as things were in Laredo, she could see that they were worse in Nuevo Laredo. She, Jovita, and four other women rushed across the Rio Grande and began pulling the wounded to safety as bullets passed near their heads. Taking as many people to the hospital as they could, the six women then assisted doctors. These courageous women risked their lives to save hundreds of people.

Wanting to do more, Jovita and Leonor created La Cruz Blanca, or the White Cross, on May 18, 1913. Upon advice from Jovita's brother Clemente, they modeled La Cruz

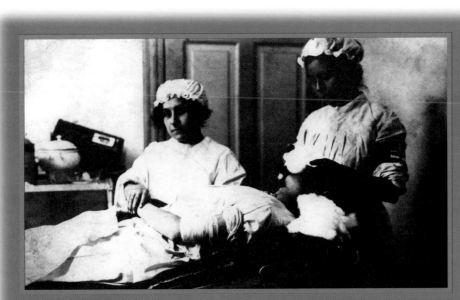

Jovita (right) and Leonor Villegas de Magnon (left) treat the wounded during the Mexican Revolution. Note that Jovita is wearing the armband of La Cruz Blanca. Jovita and Leonor created La Cruz Blanca in May 1913.

Blanca after the American Red Cross that Clara Barton started in 1881. As a nurse during the Civil War, Barton saw the need for organized emergency medical and relief services. The American Red Cross later made a difference in the lives of those the Spanish-American War affected.

Although supportive of the revolution, La Cruz Blanca was primarily a nursing corps that tended to injured soldiers on both sides and helped those near the border whom the war rendered homeless. On their left upper arms, each Cruz Blanca volunteer wore a black armband with a white cross stitched to it. Other Idar family members volunteered also. A brother, Federico, the only Idar born in Mexico, volunteered as did a sister, Elvira.

Jovita and Leonor shared an interest in education. Leonor had been operating a bilingual kindergarten from her home in Laredo. Although born in Nuevo Laredo, she attended school in San Antonio and New York. Leonor, whose nickname was La Rebelde, or the Rebel, felt strongly about helping the peasants in the Mexican Revolution. Her family inheritance supported the Revolution, and Leonor wrote about the Mexican Revolution for *La Crónica*.

On New Year's Day in 1914, another battle started in Nuevo Laredo. The battle was so intense that neither Jovita nor Leonor could make it across the river that day. Instead, they waited as injured soldiers arrived in Laredo. Some soldiers were killed as they crossed the Rio Grande. Leonor's home, once a school for Tejano children, then served as a hospital.

The nurses of La Cruz Blanca later crossed the border from El Paso into Ciudad Juárez and traveled throughout the hills of northern Mexico with the revolutionary forces Venustiano Carranza led. They risked their lives as the battles took them from Coahuila to Mexico City.

Other women traveled with the troops also, just as Aztec women had done hundreds of years ago. Women carried supplies, cooked, and fought along side the men as soldiers. These women were called adelitas. They wore a type of shawl called a rebozo as a symbol of supporting the revolution.

The Mexican Revolution was a civil war, much like the United States had experienced nearly 45 years earlier. The long revolution in Mexico led to devastation across the country. Revolutionary forces attacked on both sides of the border destroying the railroad system, crops, and livestock. A food shortage and economic chaos resulted.

People lost their homes as the war ravaged Mexico, especially northern Mexico. Nearly one million refugees fled into the United States. Not surprisingly, a large number of political refugees spilled over into Texas hoping life would be better in the United States.■

The Rio Grande River serves as the border between Mexico and Texas. Texas, long a part of Mexico, shares much history with our southern neighbor.

Jovita is shown here in the workshop of El Progreso where she worked as an editor. In 1914, El Progreso published an editorial against President Woodrow Wilson's decision to send U.S. troops to the border and their editorial brought the newspaper to the attention of federal authorities. One day, the Texas Rangers showed up to shut down El Progreso. Jovita kept the Rangers from entering, but her victory was short-lived. The Rangers returned under cover of darkness, arrested the remaining staff, and destroyed the presses.

FREEDOM OF THE PRESS

J ovita returned from her nursing duties while the Mexican Revolution raged on. She joined another Spanish language newspaper, *El Progreso*, in Laredo as an editor. In 1914, *El Progreso* published an editorial against President Woodrow Wilson's decision to send U.S. troops to the border. The editorial brought *El Progreso* to the attention of the federal authorities, and angered the U.S. government and the military.

One day Jovita heard a disturbance outside the newspaper offices and hurried to investigate. She was surprised to find Texas Rangers arriving to shut down *El Progreso*. The Texas Rangers were a law enforcement body pioneer Stephen F. Austin established in 1826 to protect settlers from Indian raids. As raids diminished and Indians either moved to Mexico or were forced onto reservations, the Rangers' duties extended to border control and tracking down horse thieves. During the 20th century, the Rangers often abused their power. They frequently treated Tejanos of south Texas violently and overstepped boundaries, as they did when trying to stop publication of *El Progreso*.

Determined to keep the press running, Jovita stood in the doorway, refusing to let the Texas Rangers enter. The U.S. Constitution guaranteed freedom of the press. Rangers by the names of Hicks, Ramsey, Chamberlain, and another ordered and threatened this small woman to move away, but she refused. With her hands firmly pressed against the door frame, she stood her ground. A crowd gathered to watch one Mexican American women stare down four armed Texas Rangers for hours. Finally, the Rangers turned around and left. People were stunned. The power of the Texas Rangers was legendary, and they had a reputation for being particularly dangerous toward Mexican Americans.

Employees in the print shop of El Progreso. Jovita is on the right.

Jovita's victory was short lived. During the darkness of night, the Rangers returned and arrested the remaining staff. With sledgehammers, they smashed the printing press and the typesetting machines. Sneaking into the offices of *El Progreso* to destroy the presses was a cowardly, yet effective act. *El Progresso* had been stopped.

But, Jovita didn't let the actions of the infamous Texas Rangers stop her. She was familiar with their brutality against Tejanos. She had heard and written about the actions of the Texas Rangers before. Tejanos called the Texas Rangers los rinches. Los rinches shot first and asked questions later.

Before Jovita was born, a group of Rangers and other Anglos killed 40 innocent Tejanos in revenge over a Mexican man killing an Anglo man from Nueces County. Such revenge killings occurred too often throughout south Texas. As the Mexican Revolution heated up, anti-Mexican sentiment worsened. Rangers participated in some of the lynching that Jovita and her family wrote about.

During Jovita's lifetime, a dramatic incident occurred. A group of Tejanos angered over mistreatment called for revolution north of the border and insisted that Texas secede from the Union. Texas Rangers put a swift stop to the plans by executing hundreds of Mexicans and Mexican Americans in the Rio Grande Valley. The Rangers forced thousands more, even American citizens of Mexican descent, across the border into Mexico.

A horrifying incident put a stop to such activities. The incident is known as the Porvenir Massacre. On January 28, 1918, Texas Rangers of Company B, Anglo ranchers, plus Troop G of the Eighth Cavalry arrived in Porvenir. Porvenir is a small community in Presidio County near Big Bend National Park at the southwestern most point of Texas. The group told people they were there to arrest outlaws who had been stealing horses and cows. While soldiers stood watch on the outskirts, Rangers and ranchers gathered up Tejano men and boys, primarily farmers and ranchers who had lived in Porvenir all their lives. The innocent men had no choice but to obey the armed men and march a mile outside of town. There, the Rangers executed 15 Tejanos.

According to Henry Warren, son-in-law of one of the victims, 42 children became orphans that day. Afterwards, Porvenir lay deserted as 140 residents fled to Mexico in fear for their lives. Porvenir ceased to exist.

Texas Governor William P. Hobby fired five of the Rangers involved in the Porvenir Massacre and ordered Company B of the Texas Rangers to disband later that year. In 1919, the Texas legislature held special hearings on Texas Ranger brutality after much pressure from Mexican government officials.

José T. Canales described the rangers misdeeds during proceedings of the joint committee of the state senate and house investigation of the Texas State Ranger Force in 1911 in Austin, Texas. Canales was a state legislator, a county judge from south Texas, and founder of the League of United Latin American Citizens (LULAC).

Canales said, "But the Rangers had established a precedent—that is, whenever a suspect was arrested they would unceremoniously execute him on the road to Brownsville or to the jail, without giving him any opportunity. Frequently we would find dead bodies, and the ranches burned. Relatives were intimidated to the extent that they would not even bury their own relatives."

The joint committee determined the Texas Rangers were responsible for killing more than 5,000 Tejanos between 1914 to 1919. Despite their misdeeds, the Rangers still exist today. Nearly 130 of them work for the state department of public safety, mainly conducting special investigations and assisting local law enforcement agencies throughout Texas.

Even though the Rangers shut down *El Progreso*, Jovita continued her work as a journalist, often as the only woman on a newspaper staff. Other Texas newspapers where she worked included *El Eco del Golfo*, or The Gulf's Edge, in Corpus Christi; *La Luz*, or The Light, in San Benito; and *La Prensa*, or The Press, in San Antonio.

Jovita continued to argue for the civil rights of all Tejanos. She fought for fairness, the lesson she learned at a young age from her father whose death she mourned on April 7, 1914. She wrote his obituary for *La Revista*, or the Review, a Masonic review with worldwide circulation her father previously published. Jovita returned to run her family's newspaper, *La Crónica*, with brothers Clemente and Eduardo. The newspaper became a true family enterprise when Jovita's sister, Elvira, and her mother took over the bookkeeping. Brothers Jose and Federico also helped out in the print shop while the three youngest Idar children, Moises, Juvencio, and Aquilino, sold issues of *La Crónica* to the public.

Another family enterprise was *Evolución*, or Evolution, a newspaper Jovita and two of her brothers started in late autumn in 1916. The newspaper continued until 1920, printing the truth about life in south Texas. The ability to write about the truth was the Idar family legacy.■

Mission San José was founded by Spanish missionaries in the 18th century. It still stands today in downtown San Antonio, a city known for its missions, including the Alamo. San Antonio has long been a major U.S. city populated and governed by Hispanic Americans.

LIFE IN SAN ANTONIO

While Jovita worked hard, she also enjoyed spending time with friends and family. One special friend was Bartolo Juárez from a prominent Laredo family. Jovita and Bartolo married on May 20, 1917. Jovita was 31 years old and ready to make some changes in her life. One of those changes was moving from Laredo to the progressive city of San Antonio. Most of the information we know about Jovita's family life in San Antonio is housed in the Woman's Collection at Texas Woman's University.

Located where the San Antonio River and San Pedro Creek meet, Spanish missionaries founded San Antonio in 1718. The city became known for its five missions, the most famous later renamed the Alamo. San Antonio was a major stronghold for Spain and later, Mexico, until Texans proclaimed their independence in 1835. Mexican soldiers briefly regained control over San Antonio in a notorious defeat at the Alamo where nearly 190 Texans died in a battle against nearly 4,000 Mexicans.

After the United States won the War with Mexico in 1848, San Antonio became and continues to be a major U.S. city. A strong haven for cultural diversity, San Antonio has long been a base for Latino activism.

When Jovita moved to San Antonio, it was also a safer location for a political activist than Laredo. Considering the actions Jovita had already taken and would continue to take, it's unlikely concerns about personal safety motivated her move. She had proven time and time again that end results mattered most, not the risks she took to achieve results.

Jovita may have settled into married life, but she didn't settle down. Believing that education was the key to ending injustice, one of the first things she did was create and operate a free bilingual kindergarten for Tejano students who might not otherwise have a chance at a good education. She was also instrumental in introducing bilingual textbooks to the Texas curriculum according to The Women's Museum in Dallas.

Although she and her husband did not have any children, Jovita was a dynamic force in the lives of her nieces and nephews, whom she often towed to political meetings. Soon seen as the family matriarch, Aunt Jovita often gave advice to family members, especially the younger ones. After the 1925 death of her sister, Elvira, in childbirth, Jovita took care of her then 2-year-old niece, Jovita Fuentes. Jovita raised her namesake the same way she was raised, with love and encouragement. The young girl learned much from her aunt, such as Latin, how to behave as a lady, and the importance of fighting for personal rights and the rights of those less fortunate than she.

San Antonio's Robert G. Green County Hospital also benefited from Jovita's boundless energy. Jovita worked as an interpreter between Spanish-speaking patients and their doctors. She also devoted time to new mothers, teaching them about hygiene and how to care for their infants.

At census time, people were likely to see the purposeful steps of Jovita as she walked the streets of Laredo and later, San Antonio, to make certain all Tejanos were counted. She worked for the census bureau during four census counts, from 1910 to 1940.

Jovita's political activities grew as she became an active member of the Democratic Party. Serving as a precinct judge for a time, she and her husband also organized El Club Democrata, or the Democrat Club, to encourage Mexican Americans to be more politically active.

Labor organization was a significant political issue affecting Mexican Americans. The mass immigration from Mexico to the U.S. during the Mexican Revolution resulted in a significant rise in migrant workers throughout the

Jovita Idar (left) with Irene Idar, Federico Idar, Concha Soberon Idar, and Jovencio Idar, taken around 1930 in San Antonio.

southwest in the 1920s. Migrant workers were used as cheap labor and required to work in unsafe conditions. Women were especially at risk. With children by their sides, women spent long days picking cotton and produce, sometimes carrying 100 pounds of cotton on their backs, before going home to take care of their families. After the stock market crash of 1929, working conditions for Chicanos worsened.

Like many others, Jovita also felt the hardships of the Great Depression of the 1930s. She was sometimes seen working at her Singer sewing machine in an effort to make ends meet.

As always, Jovita continued writing. She wrote for an Italian San Antonio newspaper, *La Voce de la Pattria.* In 1940, she became co-editor for *El Heraldo Cristiano,* or the Christian Herald, a major Spanish language publication of the Rio Grande Conference of the Methodist Church, where she also served as a conference officer. In the October 1940 issue of *El Heraldo Cristiano,* Jovita paid tribute to educators in an article called "Best Education" by writing, "Sister teacher, you have seen flashes of light budding in the eyes of some children and have felt the pleasure of understanding that you have opened the doors to knowledge for a human being."

After many years of giving, Jovita's body eventually gave out. Diabetes plagued the Idar family. At least two of Jovita's brothers died from complications of diabetes. Jovita suffered from diabetes as well as tuberculosis. She died on June 13, 1946 in San Antonio at the age of 60.

Even in death, the impact of Jovita's efforts extend far into all the areas near and dear to her heart, such as education, politics, worker's rights and particularly, rights for Latin women. Jovita's efforts inspired Latinas to help create LULAC, now the oldest ongoing civil rights organization for

Hispanic Americans in the United States. Jovita's brother, Eduardo, was one of the authors of the LULAC constitution.

Jovita's efforts also paved the way for other Latinas to make significant advances in civil rights. Emma Tenayuca, for example, of San Antonio was only 16 years old when she spoke on the steps of Finck Cigar Company about equal pay and safe working conditions. She questioned why Mexican Americans should carry the burden of poverty in a land that once belonged to Mexican people. Later in the 1930s, Tenayuca faced tear gas as she led 2,000 poorly paid pecan shellers on strike. Strikes addressed more than pay issues. Often brutal and unsafe conditions existed in the workplace. Workers might not even be allowed to use the bathroom during a 12-hour shift.

Jovita's influence wasn't limited just to Mexican American women in Texas. In New Mexico, Isabel Malgran Gonzalez organized the first strike for pea workers in New

Dolores Huerta co-founded the United Farm Workers with Cesar Chavez. Huerta was one of many Hispanic women who continued the quest for Hispanic civil rights where Idar left off.

Mexico over low pay. Dolores Huerta, another teacher, founded the United Farm Workers Union with Cesar Chavez in 1962. Meanwhile, Chicano, originally a term for unskilled Hispanic workers, evolved into a powerful and political expression for Mexican American people. The Chicano movement of the 1960s improved civil rights and political involvement for all Hispanic Americans.

Besides her impact on rights for Latinas and workers, Jovita's influence also made way for advances in politics and education. Today, record numbers of Hispanic people are seeking and winning political offices. Henry Cisneros became the first Hispanic mayor of a U.S. city when he was elected mayor of San Antonio in 1981. He later served as Secretary of Housing and Urban Development in the Clinton administration.

In the area of education, the National Hispanic Institute has taken up a cause that would make Jovita proud. Each year, the Institute holds the Lorenzo de Zavala Youth Legislation Session, an intense training conference for Latino high school seniors on the legislative and judicial powers in this county. The session places emphasis on group empowerment. According to *The Hispanic Outlook*, more than 90% of the participants go on to college.

Jovita knew firsthand about the power of education. After all, education and writing were among her life's passions. She used these tools to make the world a better place, and she lived they way she wrote, with fairness and purpose.■

CHRONOLOGY

1885   Jovita Idar born September 7 in Laredo, Texas

1903   Jovita graduates June 20 from the Holding Institute with a teaching certificate

1910   Jovita leaves teaching to write for *La Crónica*; lynching of 20-year-old Antonio Rodríguez

1911   Lynching of 14-year-old Antonio Gomez; El Primer Congreso Mexicanista holds the first Hispanic American civil rights convention in Laredo from September 14 to 22; La Liga Femenil Mexicanista is formed on October 15 and becomes the first Hispanic feminist group in the United States

1913   Along with Leonor Villegas de Magnón, Jovita creates La Cruz Blanca, an emergency nursing and disaster relief organization, on May 18

1914   Jovita blocks the Texas Rangers from entering and closing down *El Progreso*; Nicasio Idar dies April 7

1917   Jovita marries Bartolo Juárez May 20 and moves to San Antonio; Jovita creates a bilingual kindergarten

1925   Sister Elvira dies in childbirth, leaving Jovita to raise her child

1940   Jovita becomes co-editor for *El Heraldo Cristiana* in December

1946   Jovita dies on June 13 at the age of 60

TIMELINE IN HISTORY

1821   Mexico wins independence from Spain

1836   Republic of Texas forms

1845   The United States annexes Texas

1846   War with Mexico begins

1848   War ends, the United States pays Mexico $15 million for Texas to the Rio Grande, New Mexico, Arizona, California, Utah, and parts of Colorado and Wyoming; The U.S. women's suffrage movement officially begins at Seneca Falls convention

1910   Mexican Revolution begins, affecting border towns of Texas

1911   Death of Sara Estela Ramírez, a prominent activist and writer; First Hispanic civil rights convention is held, the Primer Congreso Mexicanista, and the first Hispanic feminist organization is formed, La Liga Femenil Mexicanista

1917-1918   United States involved in World War I

1918   Porvenir Massacre occurs when Texas Rangers and others kill 15 Tejanos

1920   The 19th Amendment to the U.S. Constitution passes, giving women the right to vote

1920s   Increase in migrant workers used as source of cheap labor

1929   Creation of League of United Latin American Citizens (LULAC), the oldest continually operating civil rights organization for Hispanic Americans

1929   Stock market crashes leading to the Great Depression

1938   Emma Tenayuca successfully leads 2,000 pecan shellers on strike over low pay and poor working conditions

1941-1945   United States involved in World War II

1962   Dolores Huerta and Cesar Chavez form the United Farm Workers (UFW) union

1960s   Chicano Movement works for the civil rights of all Hispanic Americans

1968   National Council of La Raza established to improve life and opportunities for all Hispanic Americans

1981   Henry Cisneros becomes the first Latino mayor of a major U.S. city

1993   President Bill Clinton appoints Cisneros Secretary of Housing and Urban Development

2002   Dolores Huerta and others continue to fight for farm labor bills; Dr. Antonia Pantoja dies May 24. Like Jovita Idar, Dr. Pantoja began as a school teacher. Both women devoted their lives to education, community and economic development and empowering the Latino communities in the United States.

FOR FURTHER READING

Berson, Robin Kadison *Marching to a Different Drummer: Unrecognized Heroes of American History*, Westport, Conn: Greenwood Press, 1994.

Gurasich, Marj *Did You Ever Meet a Texas Hero, Volume II*, Austin: Eakin Press, 1996.

Roges, Mary Beth; Smith, Sherry A.; Scott, Janelle D. *We Can Fly: Stories of Katherine Stinson and Other Gutsy Texas Women*, Austin: Ellen C. Temple, 1983.

ON THE WEB

Idar, Jovita - Handbook of Texas Online
www.tsha.utexas.edu/handbook/online/articles/view/II/fid3.html

MANA: A National Latina Organization
www.hermana.org

The Women's Museum
www.thewomensmuseum.org

GLOSSARY

abolitionist (ahb-uh-LISH-in-ist) — a person who tries to stop a practice, such as slavery

adelita (ah-duh-LEE-tuh) — a woman who marched with soldiers during the Mexican Revolution

barrio (bAR-ee-oh) — neighborhood

Chicano (chih-KAHN-oh) — person of Mexican descent who lives in the United States

civil rights — individual rights people have to freedom and equal treatment under the law

lynching (LINCH-ing) — violent death without a legal trial

precinct (PRE-sink) — an administrative district for voting or policing purposes

rebozo (rih-BOH-zoh) — a shawl or scarf that women wore who supported the Mexican Revolution

segregation (SEG-rih-GAY-shun) — the practice of keeping people or things separate from the majority group

suffrage (SUFF-rij) — the right to vote in political elections

Tejano (tay-HAHN-oh) — person of Mexican descent who lives in Texas

treaty (TREE-tee) — an agreement between governments

INDEX